If You're the Dreamer, I'm the Dream:

Selected Translations from Rilke's Book of Hours

translations by

Wally Swist

Finishing Line Press
Georgetown, Kentucky

If You're the Dreamer, I'm the Dream:

Selected Translations from
Rilke's Book of Hours

Copyright © 2025 by Wally Swist
ISBN 979-8-89990-228-4 First Edition
All rights reserved under International and Pan-American Copyright Conventions. No part of this book may be reproduced in any manner whatsoever without written permission from the publisher, except in the case of brief quotations embodied in critical articles and reviews.

ACKNOWLEDGMENTS

The Deronda Review (Special Soul Issue): *Ich bin, du Ängstlicher/Hörst du mich nicht*/I am, you fearful one

The Headlight Review (Georgia Writers): *Dein allerstes Wort war: Licht:*/Your very first word was light: Light, *Du dunkelnder Grund, geduldig ertragst du die Mauern*/You darkening ground, you patiently bear the walls, *Alles wird wieder gross sein und gewaltig*/Everything will be big and powerful again

Sunspot Lit: *Es wird nicht Ruhe in den Häusern, sei's*/It won't be quiet in the houses, be it, *Ich komme aus meinen Schwigen heim*/I return home from my silence, *Ich liebe meines Wesens Dunkelstunden*/I love the dark hours of my being, *Jetzt reifen schon die roten Berberitzen*/The red barberries are already ripening

The Woven Tale Press: *Mach mich zum Wächter deiner Weiten*/Make me the guardian of your expanses

Your Impossible Voice: "Listening to Rilke Redux" (Essay/Introduction)

Publisher: Leah Huete de Maines
Editor: Christen Kincaid
Cover Art: Odilon Redon, *Boat with Two Women in White*, pastel on paper, 1903
Author Photo: Elizabeth Wilda
Cover Design: Elizabeth Maines McCleavy
Interior Artwork: Oscar Zwintscher, *Portrait of Rainer Maria Rilke* oil on canvas, 1902

Order online: www.finishinglinepress.com
also available on amazon.com

Author inquiries and mail orders:
Finishing Line Press
PO Box 1626
Georgetown, Kentucky 40324
USA

Contents

from *The Book of Hours: The Book of The Monastic Life*

I, 1 *Da neight sich die Stunde und rührt mich an*
Then the hour approaches and touches me

I, 5 *Ich liebe meines Wesens Dunkelstunden,*
I love the dark hours of my being,

I, 11 *Du Dunkelheit, aus der ich stamme,*
You, darkness, from which I emerge,

I, 19 *Ich bin, du Ängstlicher. Hörst du mich nicht*
I am, you fearful one.

I, 44 *Dein allerstes Wort war: Licht:*
Your very first word was: Light:

I, 50 *Ich komme aus meinen Schwigen heim,*
I return home from my silence,

I, 52 *Mein Leben hat das gleiche Kleid und Haar*
My life is not this steep hour,

I, 59 *Gott spricht zu jedem nur, eh er ihn macht,*
God speaks to each one of us, before he makes us,

I, 61 *Du dunkelnder Grund, geduldig erträgst du die Mauern.*
You darkening ground, you patiently bear the walls.

I, 62 . . . *Ich danke dir, du tiefe Kraft,*
. . . I thank you, immeasurable strength

from *The Book of Hours: The Book of Pilgrimage*

II, 11 . . . *Keiner lebt sein Leben.*
. . . No one lives their life.

II, 12 *Und doch, obwohl ein jeder von sich strebt*
And yet, although everyone strives for themselves,

II, 22 Du bist die Zukunft, großes Morgenrot
You are the future, great dawn

II, 25 Alles wird wieder groß sein und gewaltig.
Everything will be big and powerful again.

II, 27 Es wird nicht Ruhe in den Häusern, sei's
It won't be quiet in the houses, be it

II, 29 Du Gott, ich moechte viele Pilger sein,
God, I want to be many pilgrims,

II, 30 Bei Tag bist du das Hoerensagen,
By day you are the whispering

II, 32 Jetzt reifen schon die roten Berberitzen,
The red barberries are already ripening,

I, 34 In tiefen Naechten grab ich dich, du Schatz.
In deep nights, I'll dig for you, beloved.

        from *The Book of Hours: The Book of Poverty and Death*

III, 1 Vielleicht, daß ich durch schwere Berge gehe
Perhaps, I walk through massive mountains

III, 3 Mach mich zum Wächter deiner Weiten,
Make me the guardian of your expanses,

III. 6 O Herr, gieb jedem seinen eignen Tod.
O Lord, grant everyone their own death.

III, 7 Denn wir sind nur die Schale und das Blatt.
Because we are only the shell and the leaf,

III, 12 Und gibe, daß beide Stimmen mich begleiten,
And give both voices to accompany me

III, 13 Die großen Stadte sind nicht wahr; sie tauschen
The rough cities are untrue, they betray

III, 19 Du, der du weißt, und dessen weites Wissen
You, who know, and whose vast knowledge

III, 20 Betrachte sie und sieh, was ihnen gliche:
Look at them and see what they resemble:

III, 29 Nur nimm sie wieder aus der Städte Schuld,
Only take them out of the cities' debt again,

III, 32 Und deine Armen leiden unter diesen
And your poor suffer from these

III, 34 O wo ist er, der Klare, hingeklungen?
Oh, where is he, where has the clear one gone?

Author's Biographical Note

Translator's Biographical Note

Listening to Rilke Redux

I first began reading Rainer Maria Rilke in the autumn of 1973, when I was twenty. His work filled me as few other poets would both then and in the decades to follow. I read widely. My list of favorites grew as I read even more: Jacobsen, Jimenez, Lorca, Milosz, Neruda, Trakl. Yes, they were often poets found in translation. However, I also did have my list of American poets, such as Jack Gilbert, Donald Hall, Robert Francis, Mary Oliver, among a host of others.

Rilke, though, held me, opened up to me in various rereading. His mysticism was not only attractive but I also saw it as a possible path on which I could learn to guide my own life. I never saw Rilke's angels but I could feel the presence of my own.

Another attribute in my early reading of Rilke was that I knew Stephen Mitchell, when he was a grad student at Yale. Stephen would often stop me in the street, between classes, to show me his most recent Rilke translations. He would open his briefcase and pull out newly typed translations and read some lines to me, first in German, then in English, to illustrate how musical Rilke sounded in German, and how he was trying to cast a similar lyricism in English.

Decades since, in October 2017, I revisited Rilke, as I often have over the years, in my rereading of *The Duino Elegies* and *The Orpheus Sonnets*. The sequences availed themselves to me as they had never done before. I experienced a mystical breakthrough in my reading of the work. This resulted in my writing a couple of tribute poems to Rilke, "Two Echoes for Rilke" and "Rilke, at the Chateau de Muzot." This was followed by my translating a poem from *The Orpheus Sonnets*, Part Two, XII.

In the summer of 2018, I had another mystical experience in my reading Rilke. Doors opened where I wasn't aware any doors were. I came upon C. F. McIntyre's 1947 translation of Rilke's *Das Marienleben, or The Life of the Virgin Mary*, a sequence of thirteen poems of various lengths. The sequence was composed by Rilke in 1900 during his Worpswede art colony years. This was before his years spent under the aesthetic tutelage of Rodin, as his personal secretary. This was on the cusp of the Romanticism of the 19th-century and the modernism of the 20th-century.

I have admired many translators of the poetry of Rainer Maria Rilke. Of course, there are Stephen Mitchell's translations, many of which I was graced to see in early drafts. I also have admired Edward

Snow's work, and more recently, an erudite poet and translator from San Francisco, Art Beck's versions, especially, of *The Orpheus Sonnets*, which are as crisp and vital as they are vehicles for Rilke's angelic visions and poetic rapture.

However, there were poems such as the ones included here which nearly tacitly spoke to me audibly. The words and the images opened to me as a poem of my own would—but with Rilkean splendor. I had to rush to write down what I was hearing, and it seemed, at least at the time, that I was also listening to my inner angel.

The intent of this book is for it to offer praise to the poet who cited praise as the highest form of poetry. In Rilke's praises, we find our own praise—of ourselves, of others, of mostly anything, actually. When anyone experiences an epiphany that person wants to share that epiphany. When you have experienced many, it is really nearly an imperative that others know and hear the song, or songs, that have led to the opening of the light.

May my interpretative adaptations become threads woven into the fabric of the work of Rainer Maria Rilke in English. May it lead to exploring Rilke's major works as fully as any reader can—which demand, for many reasons, a multitude of rereadings. The work contained here led me to my own experience of what is mystical and to further it. May this same work open for you in a similar way and provide nurture and sustenance, as it has for me.

However, what I have found continually in the many rereadings of Rilke's *The Book of Hours* is best stated by Wolfgang Leppmann in his inestimably valuable biography of Rilke, entitled *Rilke: A Life* (New York: Fromm International, 1984). This paragraph is quoted from page 115:

"With the *New Poems*, the *Duino Elegies*, and the *Sonnets to Orpheus, the Book of Hours* is one of the masterworks of modern German poetry. It's title is taken from the "livres d'heures," breviaries compiled for lay worship and often ornamented with means of structuring the devotional day. Taken together, Rilke's poems do represent a spiritual journal . . . The sense of breviary is underscored by a fictional device that is followed consistently in the first book, sporadically preserved in the second, and abandoned in the third: the individual poems are in fact prayers being recorded by a Russian monk in his cell."

With this in mind, translating such a work into English is a humbling task. Although, as Leppmann posits, the quality of the lyric is masterful, and taken with Rilke's early insights into spirituality, since these were poems written when he was still a young man, aim high to articulate what is the unspoken inviolate streaming of the deep and expansive spirit, so to attempt to translate that into English is to craft, at best, as a translator, Rilke's inner angel as well as yours and mine, so the difficulty is in each detail, and angels, as we well know, love to dance on the head of a pin.

Wally Swist
South Hadley, Massachusetts

Dedication by Rainer Maria Rilke:

Gelegt in die Haende von Lou

To Lou Andreas Salome

Translator's Dedication:

Gelegt in die Haende von Tevis

To Tevis Kimball

from *The Book of Hours:*
The Book of The Monastic Life

I, 1

*Da neight sich die Stunde und rührt mich an
mit klarem, metallenem Schlag:
mit zittern die Sinne. Ich fühle: ich kann—
und ich fasse den plastischen Tag.*

*Nichts war noch vollendet, eh ich es erschaut,
ein jedes Werden stand still.
Meine Blicke sind reif, und wie eine Braut
kommt jedem das Ding, das er will . . .*

I, 1

Da neight sich die Stunde und rührt mich an

Then the hour approaches and touches me
with a clear, sharp blow:
my senses ring with it. I feel it: I can—
and I grasp the shape of the day.

Nothing was finished before my awareness of it,
every becoming was stilled.
My vision ripens things
and they come toward me, like a bride, to be met . . .

I, 5

Ich liebe meines Wesens Dunkelstunden,
in welchen meine Sinne sich vertiefen;
in ihnen hab ich, wie in alten Briefen,
mein täglich Leben schon gelebt gefunden
und wie Legende weit und überwunden.

Aus ihnen kommt mir Wissen, daß ich Raum
zu einem zweiten zeitlos breiten Leben habe.

Und manchmal bin ich wie der Baum,
der, reif und rauschend, über einem Grabe
den Traum erfüllt, den der vergangne Knabe
(um en sich seine warmen Wurzeln drängen)
verlor in Traurigkeiten und Gesängen.

I, 5

Ich liebe meines Wesens Dunkelstunden

I love the dark hours of my being,
in which my senses deepen;
in them, as in old letters,
I have found my daily life already lived,
and, like a legend, far and subdued.

From them comes knowledge that I have space
for a second timelessly broad life.

And sometimes I'm like the tree
that, ripe and rustling, over a grave
fulfills the dream that the boy who died
(around whom its warm roots crowd)
lost in sadness and song.

I, 11

*Du Dunkelheit, aus der ich stamme,
ich liebe dich mehr als die Flamme,
welche die Welt begrenzt,
indem sie glänzt
fur irend einen Kreis,
aus dem heraus kein Wesen von ihr weiß.*

*Aber die Dunkelheit hält alles an sich:
Gestalten und Flammen, Tiere und mich,
wie sie's errafft,
Menschen und Mächte—*

*Und es kann sein: eine große Kraft
ruhrt sich in meiner Nachbarschaft.*

Ich glaube an Nächte.

I, 11

Du Dunkelheit, aus der ich stamme

You, darkness, from which I emerge,
I love you more than the flame,
which limits the world
by illuminating
for everyone a circle,
out of which no being knows about.

But the darkness holds everything in itself.
Shapes and flames, animals and myself,
Peoples and Powers
just as they are.

And it just could be: that a great power
is stirring in my neighborhood.

I believe in night.

I, 19

Ich bin, du Ängstlicher. Hörst du mich nicht
mit allen meinen Sinnen an dir branden?
Meine Gefühle, welche Flügel fanden,
umkreisen weiß dein Angesicht.
Siehst du nicht meine Seele, wie sie dicht
vor dir in einem Kleid aus Stille steht?
Reift nicht mein mailiches Gebet
an deinem Blicke wie an einem Baum?

Wenn du der Träumer bist, bin ich dein Traum.
Doch wenn du wachen willst, bin ich dein Wille
mächtig aller Herrlichkeit
und mich mächtig aller Herrlichkeitx
und ründe werde wie eine Sternenstille
über der wunderlichen Stadt der Zeit.

I, 19

Ich bin, du Ängstlicher. Hörst du mich nicht

I am, you fearful one.
Do you not hear me burn against you
with all my senses? My feelings that found
wings encircle your knowing face.
And don't you see my soul standing before you
in a dress of silence?
And isn't my spring prayer ripening
inside you like fruit on a tree?

If you're the dreamer, I'm the dream.
But if you want to wake up, I am your will
and powerful in all glory
and round me like a starry stillness
over the whimsical city of time.

I, 44

Dein allerstes Wort war: Licht:
da ward die Zeit, Dann schwiegst du lange
Dein zweites Wort ward Mensch und bange
(wir dunkeln noch in seinem Klange)
und wieder sinnt dein Angesicht.

Ich aber will dein drittes nicht.

Ich bete nachts oft: Sei de Stumme,
der waschend in Gebärden bleibt
und den der Geist im Traume treibt,
daß er des Schwiegens schwere Summe
in Stirnen und Gebirge schreibt.

Sei du die Zuflucht vor dem Zorne,
der das Unsagbare verstieß.
Es wurde Nacht im Paradies:
sei du der Huter mit dem Horne,
und man erzahlt nur, daß er blies.

I, 44

Dein allerstes Wort war: Licht:

Your very first word was: *Light*:
with that there was time, then you were long silent.
Your second word became man and fear
(we still darken in its sound)
and again your face reflects this.

But I don't want your third.

I often pray at night: be mute,
who remains washing in gestures,
and whom the spirit drives in dreams,
that he writes the heavy sum of silence
on foreheads and mountains.

Be thou the refuge from wrath,
who violated the unspeakable.
It was night in paradise:
be you the keeper with the horn,
and one only says, that he blew.

I, 50

Ich komme aus meinen Schwigen heim,
mit denen ich mich verlor.
Ich war Gesang, und Gott, der Reim,
rauscht noch in meinem Ohr.

Ich werde weider still und schlicht,
und meine Stimme steht;
es senkte sich mein Angesicht
zu besserem Gebet.
Den andern war ich wie ein Wind,
da ich sie ruttelnd rief.
Weit war ich, wo die Engel sind,
hoch, wo das Licht in Nichts zerrinnt--
Gott aber dunkelt tief...

I, 50

Ich komme aus meinen Schwigen heim,

I return home from my silence,
within which I lost myself.
I was the singer, and God, the rhyme,
still resounding in my ears.

I will be quiet and simple,
and my voice stands;
my face lowers
to ardent prayer.
To the others I was like the wind,
as I called her trembling.
I was far away from where the angels are,
high, where the light melts into nothingness—
But deeply dark in God.

I, 52

Mein Leben hat das gleiche Kleid und Haar,
wie aller alten Zaren Sterbestunde.
Die Macht entfremdete nur meinem Munde,
doch meine Reiche, die ich schweigend runde,
versammeln sich in meinem Hintergrunde
und meine Sinne sind noch Gossudar.

Fur sie ist beten immer noch: Erbauen,
aus allen Maßen baueen, daß dad Grauen
fast wie die Größe wird und schon,—
und: jedes Hinknien und Vertrauen
(daß es die andern nicht beschauen)
mit vielen goldenen und blauen
und bunten Kuppeln überhöhn . . .

I, 52

Mein Leben hat das gleiche Kleid und Haar,

My life is not this steep hour,
where you see me hurrying.
I am a tree against my background,
I am just one of my many mouths
and the one that closes first.

I am the silence between two tones
that only get used to each with difficulty:
because the sound of death wants to rise—
but in the dark interval both are reconciled, trembling.
And the song stays beautiful.

I, 59

Gott spricht zu jedem nur, eh er ihn macht,
dann geht er schweigend mit ihm aus der Nacht.
Aber die Worte, eh jeder beginnt,
diese wolkigen Worte, sind:

Von deinen Sinnen hinausgesandt,
geh bis an deiner Sehnsucht Rand;
gieb mir Gewand.
Hinter den Dingen wachse als Brand,
daß ihre Schatten, ausgespannt,
immer mich ganz bedecken.

Laß dir Alles geschehn: Schönheit un Schrecken.
Man muß nur gehn: Kein Gefuhl ist das fernste.
Laß dich von mir nicht trennen.
Nah ist das Land,
das sie das Leben nennen.

Du wirst es erkennen
an seinem Ernste.

Geb mir die Hand.

I, 59

Gott spricht zu jedem nur, eh er ihn macht,

God speaks to each one of us, before he makes us,
then he silently goes with us out of the night.
But the words before everyone begins,
those cloudy words, are:

you, sent out beyond your senses,
lean out to the edge of your longing;
manifest me.
Flare up as a flame
so that their shadows, stretched out,
always cover me completely.

Allow everything to happen to you: beauty and horror.
All you have to do is to keep going:
no feeling is the ultimate.
Don't let me separate you.
The land is near,
that is called life.

You will recognize it
by its seriousness.

Give me your hand.

I, 61

Du dunkelnder Grund, geduldig ertragst du die Mauern.
Und vielleicht erlaubst du noch eine Stunde den Stadten zu dauern
und gewahrst noch zwei Stunden den Kirchen und einsamen Klöstern
und lassest funf Stunden noch Mühsal allen Erlöstern
und siehst noch sieben Stunden das Tagwerk des Bauern—:

Eh du wieder Wald wirst und Wasser und Wachsende Wildnis
in der Stunde der unerfaßlichen Angst,
da du dein unvollendetes Bildnis
von allen Dingen zurückverlangst.

Gieb mir noch eine kleine Weile Zeit: ich will die Dinge
so wie keiner lieben
bis sie dir würdig sind und weit.

Ich will nur sieben Tabe, sieben
auf die sich keiner noch geschrieben,
Sieben Seiten Einsamkeit.

Wem du das Buch giebst, welches die umfaßt,
der wird gebückt über den Blättern bleiben.
Es sei denn, daß du ihn in Händen hast,
um, selbst zu schreiben.

I, 61

Du dunkelnder Grund, geduldig erträgst du die Mauern.

You darkening ground, you patiently bear the walls.
And maybe you allow another hour to last in the cities
and you still allow two hours in the churches and remote monasteries
and leave five hours of hardship to all redeemed
and see the daily work of the farmer for another seven hours—

before you become forest again and water and growing wilderness
in the hour of incomprehensible fear,
since you are your unfinished image
reclaimed from all things.

Give me a little more time: I want to love things
like no loves them
until they are all worthy of you and far.

I just want seven days, seven
of which no one has written yet,
seven pages of solitude.

To whom you give that book
that contains them will remain bent, over the leaves.
Unless you have them, in your hands,
to write yourself through them.

I, 62

. . . Ich danke dir, du tiefe Kraft,
die immer leiser mit mir schafft
wie hinter vielen Wänden;
jetzt ward mir erst der Werktag sclicht
und wie ein heiliges Geisicht
zu meinen dunklen Händen.

I, 62

. . . Ich danke dir, du tiefe Kraft

. . . I thank you, immeasurable strength
that works within me ever more quietly
as if behind many walls;
now the day's labor finally clears for me,
and like a holy face
to hold in my dark hands.

from *The Book of Hours:*
The Book of Pilgrimage

II, 11

. . . Keiner lebt sein Leben.
Zufälle sind die Menschen, Stimmen, Stucke,
Alltage, Ängste, viele kleine Glüecke,
verkleidet schon als Kinder, eingemummt,
Als Masken mundig, als Gesicht—verstummt.

Ich denke oft: Schätzhauser mussen sein,
wo alle diese vielen Leben liegen
wie Panzer oder Sänften oder Wiegen,
in welche nie ein Wirklicher gestiegen,
und wie Geväwnder, welche ganz allein
nicht stehen können und sich sinkend schmiegen
an starke Wände aus gewölbtem Stein.

Und wenn ich abends immer weiterginge
aus meinem Garten, drin ich müde bin,—
ich weiß: dann führen alle Wege hin
zum Arsenal der ungelebten Dinge . . .

II, 11

. . . Keiner lebt sein Leben.

. . . No one lives their life.
People, voices, pieces, everyday life,
fears, the many occasions of luck
are but coincidences,
disguised as children, wrapped up,
mature as masks, as a face—silent.

I often think: treasure houses must be
where many of these lives lie
like armor or soft things or cradles,
into which no real man ever climbed,
and like clothes that cannot stand all alone,
and sinking, nestle against
strong walls of arched stone.

And if I kept walking in the evenings
in my garden, in which I am tired,—
I know: all the roads lead there
to the arsenal of all unlived things . . .

II,12

*Und doch, obwohl ein jeder von sich strebt
wie aus dem Kerker, der ihn hasst und halt,—
es ist ein großes Wunder in der Welt:
ich fuehle: alles Leben wird gelebt.*

*Wer lebt es denn? Sind das die Dinge, die
wie eine ungespielte Melodie
im Abend wie in einer Harfe stehn?
Sind das die Winde, die von Wassern wehn,
sind das die Zweige, die sich Zeichen geben,
sind das die Blumen, die dir Düefte weben,
sind das die langen alternden Alleen?
Sind das die warmen Tiere, welche gehn,
sind das die Vögel, die sich fremd erheben?*

Wer lebt es denn? Lebst du es, Gott,—das Leben?

II, 12

Und doch, obwohl ein jeder von sich strebt

And yet, although everyone strives for themselves,
as from the prison that keeps them,—
there is an immense wonder in the world:
I feel: all life is being lived.

Who lives there? Are these the things, that
like an unplayed melody,
await in the evening like a harp?
Are these the winds that blow in from off the waters?
Are these the branches that signal themselves?
Are these the flowers that weave their scents?
Are these the long aging avenues?
Are these the warm animals that pass?
Are these the birds that rise up strangely?

Who lives there? Are you living it, God,—this life?

II, 22

Du bist die Zukunft, großes Morgenrot
über den Ebenen der Ewigkeit.
Du bist der Hahnschrei nach der Nact der Zeit,
der Tau die Morgenmette und die Maid,
der fremde Mann, die Mutter und der Tod.

Du bist die sich verwandelnde Gestalt,
die immer einsam aud dem Schicksal ragt,
die unbejubelt bleibt und unbeklagt
und unbeschrieben wie ein wilder Wald.

Du bist der Dinge Tiefer Inbegriff,
der seinse Wesens letztes Wort verschweigt
und sich den Andern immer anders zeigt:
dem Schiff als Küste und dem Land als Schiff.

II, 22

Du bist die Zukunft, großes Morgenrot

You are the future, great dawn
above levels of adversity.
You are the cock's crow after a night's close,
the dew, matins, the maiden,
the stranger, the mother, and death.

You are the transformative figure,
who always stands alone in fate
that remains uncelebrated and without complaints
and that is undescribed like a wild forest.

You are the fathomless embodiment of things,
who hides his last word
and always shows himself differently to others:
the ship as coast and the coast as ship.

II, 25

Alles wird wieder groß sein und gewaltig.
Die Lande einfach und die Wasser faltig,
die Bäume riesig und sehr klein die Mauern;
und in den Tälern, stark und vielgestaltig,
ein Volk von Hirten und von Ackerbauern.

Und keine Kirchen, welche Gott umklammern
wie einen Flüchtling und ihn dann bejammern
wie ein gefangenes und wundes Tier, -
die Haeuser gastlich allen Einlaßklopfern
und ein Gefhl von unbegrenztem Opfern
in allem Handeln und in dir und mir.

Kein Jenseitswarten und kein Schaun nach drueben,
nur Sehnsucht, auch den Tod nicht zu entweihn
und dienend sich am Irdischen zu üben,
um seinen Händen nicht mehr neu zu sein.

II, 25

Alles wird wieder groß sein und gewaltig.

Everything will be big and powerful again.
The land is plain and the water is rippled,
the trees huge and the walls small;
and in the valleys strong and varied,
people who are shepherds and tillers of the soil.

And no churches embracing God
like a refugee and then a lament for him,
like a trapped and wounded animal,—
the houses hospitable to all the knockers,
and a sense of unlimited sacrifice
in all actions, and in you and me.

No waiting for the afterlife and no looking beyond,
only longing not only to profane death
but to also practice on the earthly,
so as to no longer be new to his hands.

II, 27

*Es wird nicht Ruhe in den Häusern, sei's
daß einer stirbt und sie ihn weitertragen,
sei es daß wer auf heimliches Geheiß
den Pilgerstock nimmt und den Pilgerkragen,
um in der Fremde nach dem Weg zu fragen,
auf welchem er dich warten weiß.*

*Die Straßen werden derer niemals leer,
die zu dir wollen wie zu jener Rose,
die alle tausend Jahre einmal blüht.
Viel dunkles Volk und beinah Namenlose,
und wenn sie dich erreichen, sind sie müd.*

*Aber ich habe ihren Zug gesehn;
und glaube seither, daß die Winde wehn
aus ihren Mänteln, welche sich bewegen,
und stille sind wenn sie sich niederlegen—;
so groß war in den Ebenen ihr Gehn.*

II, 27

Es wird nicht Ruhe in den Häusern, sei's

It won't be quiet in the houses, be it
that one dies and they carry him on,
be it that on secret command someone
takes the pilgrim's stick and collar
to ask for the way abroad,
on which he knows you are waiting.

The streets will never be empty
of those who want to see you as that rose
which blooms once every thousand years.
Many dark people are almost nameless,
and when they reach you they are tired.

But I have seen the procession;
and have believed ever since that the winds blow
from the movement of their cloaks,
and are silent when they lie down—:
so great is their walking in the plains.

II, 29

Du Gott, ich moechte viele Pilger sein,
um so, ein langer Zug, zu dir zu gehn,
und um ein grosses Stueck von dir zu sein:
du Garten mit den lebenden Alleen.
Wenn ich so gehe wie ich bin, allein, -
wer merkt es denn? Wer sieht mich zu dir gehn?
Wen reisst es hin? Wen regt es auf, und wen
bekehrt es dir?

Als waere nichts geschehn,
— lachen sie weiter. Und da bin ich froh,
dass ich so gehe wie ich bin; denn so
kann keiner von den Lachenden mich sehn.

II, 29

Du Gott, ich moechte viele Pilger sein

God, I want to be many pilgrims,
and like that, can be a long procession to you,
and in that way be a large part of you:
you, garden with living avenues.
When I walk as I am, I am alone,—
who notices? Who sees me going to you?
Who cares? Whom does it upset?
Whom does it bring to you?

As if nothing had happened,
—they keep laughing. And I'm glad,
that I go as I am; because like that
none of those laughing can see me.

II, 30

Bei Tag bist du das Hoerensagen,
das fluesternd um die Vielen fliesst;
die Stille nach dem Stundenschlagen,
welche sich langsam wieder schliesst.

Jemehr der Tag mit immer schwaechern
Gebaerden sich nach Abend neigt,
jemehr bist du, mein Gott. Es steigt
dein Reich wie Rauch aus allen Daechern.

II, 30

Bei Tag bist du das Hoerensagen

By day you are the whispering
that flows around the many,
the silence after the hour strikes,
which is slowly closing.

The day, with always weaker gestures,
tends towards evening, the more
you are, my God. Your kingdom
is rising like smoke from every roof.

II, 32

Jetzt reifen schon die roten Berberitzen,
alternde Astern atmen schwach im Beet.
Wer jetzt nicht reich ist, da der Sommer geht,
wird immer warten und sich nie besitzen.

Wer jetzt nicht seine Augen schliessen kann,
gewiss, dass eine Fuelle von Gesichten
in ihm nur wartet bis die Nacht begann,
um sich in seinem Dunkel aufzurichten—:
der ist vergangen wie ein alter Mann.

Dem kommt nichts mehr, dem stoesst kein Tag mehr zu,
und alles luegt ihn an, was ihm geschieht;
auch du, mein Gott. Und wie ein Stein bist du,
welcher ihn taeglich in die Tiefe zieht.

II, 32

Jetzt reifen schon die roten Berberitzen

The red barberries are already ripening,
aging asters breathe feebly in their bed.
Those who are not rich now that summer is gone,
will always wait and never own themselves.

Those who can't close their eyes now,
certain that a wealth of visions in it
only waits until the night begins,
to rise up in its darkness—:
passes on like an old man.

Nothing will come to him, no more days will be allotted,
and everything that occurs is a deception to him;
you, too, my God. And you are like a stone
that pulls him down every day.

II, 34

In tiefen Naechten grab ich dich, du Schatz.
Denn alle Ueberflüsse, die ich sah,
sind Armut und armsaeliger Ersatz
fuer deine Schönheit, die noch nie geschah.

Aber der Weg zu dir ist furchtbar weit
und, weil ihn lange keiner ging, verweht.
O du bist einsam. Du bist Einsamkeit,
du Herz, das zu entfernten Talen geht.

Und meine Hände, welche blutig sind
vom Graben, heb ich offen in den Wind,
so dass sie sich verzweigen wie ein Baum.
Ich sauge dich mit ihnen aus dem Raum

als hättest du dich einmal dort zerschellt
in einer ungeduldigen Gebärde,
und fielest jetzt, eine zerstäubte Welt,
aus fernen Sternen wieder auf die Erde
sanft wie ein Frühlingsregen faellt.

II, 34

In tiefen Naechten grab ich dich, du Schatz

In deep nights, I'll dig for you, beloved.
For all the abundance I saw
is poverty and a pitiful substitute
for your beauty that never happened.

But the way to you is terribly long,
and because no one has walked it for a long time,
it is obscured. Oh you are solitary,
you are solitude itself, dear heart,
that occupies distant valleys.

And my hands, which are bloodied
from digging, I lift open to the wind,
so that they branch out like a tree.
I'll draw you out of space with them,

as if you had yourself shattered there once
in an impatient gesture,
and fell now, an atomized world,
from distant stars back to earth
soft as a rainfall in spring.

from *The Book of Hours:*
The Book of Poverty and Death

III, 1

*Vielleicht, daß ich durch schwere Berge gehe
in harten Adern, wie ein Erz allein:
und bin so tief, daß ich kein Ende sehe
und keine Ferne: alles wurde Nähe
und alle Nähe wurde Stein.*

*Ich bin ja noch kein Wissender im Wehe,—
so macht mich dieses große Dunkel klein:
bist Du es aber: mach dich schwer, brich ein:
daß deine ganze Hand an mire geschehe
und ich an dir mit meinem ganzen Schrein.*

III, 1

Vielleicht, daß ich durch schwere Berge gehe

Perhaps, I walk through massive mountains
in hard veins, like an ore, alone:
and am so deep I can't see the end
and no distance: everything became near
and all the nearness became stone.

I am not yet a knower of pain,—
so this great darkness makes me small;
but if it is *you*, make yourself difficult, break in:
that your whole hand may hold me,
and that I hold you with my whole cry.

III, 3

Mach mich zum Wächter deiner Weiten,
mach mich zum Horchenden am Stein,
gib mir die Augen auszubreiten
auf deiner Meere Einsamsein;
laß mich der Flüsse Gang begleiten
aus dem Geschrei zu beiden Seiten
weit in den Klang der Nacht hine
in. Schick mich in deine leeren Länder,
durch die weiten Winde gehn,
wo große Klöster wie Gewänder
um ungelebte Leben stehn.
Dort will ich mich zu Pilgern halten,
von ihren Stimmen und Gestalten
durch keinen Trug mehr abgetrennt,
und hinter einem blinden Alten
des Weges gehn, den keiner kennt.

III, 3

Mach mich zum Wächter deiner Weiten,

Make me the guardian of your expanses,
make me listener at the stone,
let me open my eyes
to your seas of loneliness;
let me accompany the flow of the river
from the shouts on both sides
far into the sound of the night.
Send me to your empty lands,
through which the far winds go,
where great monasteries
stand like robes around unlived lives.
There I want to join with pilgrims,
of their voice and forms
no longer separated by deceit,
and behind a blind old man
go the way no one knows.

III. 6

O Herr, gieb jedem seinen eignen Tod.
Das Sterben, das aus jenem Leben geht,
darin er Liebe hatte, Sinn und Not.

III, 6

O Herr, gieb jedem seinen eignen Tod.

O Lord, grant everyone their own death.
The dying that emerges from a life
in how we loved, what was our intent, our need.

III, 7

Denn wir sind nur die Schale und das Blatt.
Der große Tod, den jeder in sich hat,
das ist die Frucht, um die sich alles dreht . . .

III, 7

Denn wir sind nur die Schale und das Blatt.

Because we are only the shell and the leaf,
the great death that we all carry with us
is the fruit around which everything else revolves . . .

III, 12

Und gibe, daß beide Stimmen mich begleiten,
streust du mich wieder aus in Stadt und Angst.
Mit ihnen will ich sein im Zorn der Zeiten,
und dir aus meinem Klang ein Bett bereiten
an jeder Stelle wo du es verlangst.

III, 12

Und gibe, daß beide Stimmen mich begleiten,

And give both voices to accompany me
when you scatter me again into the city and in fear.

I want to be with them in the fury of our times
and help me prepare a bed for you when I call to you

wherever you need, anywhere you ask.

III, 13

*Die großen Stadte sind nicht wahr; sie tauschen
den Tag, die Nact, die Tiere und das Kind;
ihr Schweigen lügt, sie lügen mit Geräuschen
und mit den Dingen, welche willig sind.*

*Nichts von dem weiten wirklichen Geschehen,
das sich um dich, du Werdender, bewegt,
geschieht in ihnen. Diener Winde Wehen
fallt in die Gassen, die es anders drehen,
ihr Rauschen wird im Hin-und Wiedergehen
verwirrt, gereizt und aufgeregt . . .*

III, 13

Die großen Stadte sind nicht wahr; sie tauschen

The rough cities are untrue, they betray
the day, the night, animals, and the child;
their silence is a lie, they lie with their noise
and with the things that let themselves be used.

Nothing of what truly happens, that moves
around you, your becoming, happens in them.
In your streets, your wind blows, churning
amid the frenzy of traffic
and as it moves back and forth
becomes irritated, electrified, confused ...

III, 19

*Du, der du weißt, und dessen weites Wissen
aus Armut ist und Armutsüberfluß:
Mach, daß die Armen nicht mehr fortgeschmissen
und eingetreten werden in Verdruß.
Die andern Menschen sind wie ausgerissen;
sie aber stehn wie eine Blumen-Art
aus Wurzeln auf und duften wie Melissen,
und ihre Blätter sind gezackt und zart.*

III, 19

Du, der du weißt und dessen weites Wissen

You, who know, and whose vast knowledge
is out of poverty and the abundance of poverty:
make sure the poor aren't thrown away anymore
and be entered into affliction.
The other people appear as if they are torn out;
but they arise like a kind of flower
from the roots and smell like lemon balm,
and their leaves are jagged and delicate.

III, 20

Betrachte sie und sieh, was ihnen gliche:
sie rühren sich wie in den Wind gestellt
und ruhen aus wie etwas, was man hält.
In ihren Augen ist das feierliche
Verdunkeltwerden lichter Wiesenstriche,
auf die ein rascher Sommerregen fällt.

III, 20

Betrachte sie und sieh, was ihnen gliche.

Look at them and see what they resemble:
they move as if they are exposed to the wind,
they rest as if they are held by unseen hands.
In their eyes there is a celebratory darkening
over bright patches of meadow
upon which a quick summer rain falls.

III, 29

Nur nimm sie wieder aus der Städte Schuld,
wo ihnen alles Zorn ist und verworren
und wo sie in den Tagen aus Tumult
verdorren mit verwundeter Geduld.

Hat denn für sie die Erde Keinen Raum?
Wen sucht der Wind? Wer trinkt des Baches Helle?
Ist in der Teiche tiefem Ufertraum
kein Spiegelbild mehr frie fur Tur und Schwelle?
Sie brauchen ja nur eine Kleine Stelle,
auf der sie alles haben wie ein Baum.

III, 29

Nut nimm sie wieder aus der Stadte Schuld,

Only take them out of the cities' debt again,
where all is wrath and confusion
and where they are in the days of turmoil
wither with wondering patience.

Does the earth have no room for them?
Who is the wind seeking? Who drinks the light of the brook?
Is the pond deep dreaming of the shore
no more reflection free for door and threshold?
They only need a small spot, like a tree,
where they might have everything.

III, 32

Und deine Armen leiden unter diesen
und sind von allem, was sie schauen, schwer
und glühen frierend wie in Fieberkrisen
und gehn, aus jeder Wohnung ausgewiesen,
wie fremde Tote in der Nacht umher;
und sind beladen mit dem ganzen Schmutze
und wie in Sonne Faulendes bespien,—
von jedem Zufall, von der Dirnen Putze,
von Wagen und Laternen angeschrien.

Und gibt es einen Mund zu ihrem Schutze,
so mach ihn mündig und bewege ihn.

III. 32

Und deine Armen leiden unter diesen

And your poor suffer from these
and are heavy from all that they hold,
and glow freezing as in fever crisis, and go
expelled from every dwelling,
like dead strangers wandering around in the night;
and are all laden with the filth,
and like spatting on some things rotting in sun,—
from every coincidence, from the harlot's plaster,
screamed at by wagons and lanterns.

And if there is a mouth to protect them,
so make it open and speak.

III, 34

O wo ist er, der Klare, hingeklungen?
Was fühlen ihn, den Jubelnden und Jungen,
die Armen, welche harren, nicht von fern?

Was steight er nicht in ihre Dämmerungen—
der Armut großer Abendstern.

III, 34

O wo ist er, der Klare, hingeklungen?

Oh, where is he, where has the clear one gone?
Do the poor, who await for him from afar,
feel him among them, the rejoicing and youthful one?

Why doesn't he rise into their twilights—
Poverty's great evening star?

Oscar Zwintscher, *Portrait of Rainer Maria Rilke* oil on canvas, 1902

René Karl Wilhelm Johann Josef Maria Rilke (4 December 1875—29 December 1926), better known as **Rainer Maria Rilke**, was an Austrian poet and novelist. Rilke is appreciated as one of the most lyrical German-language poets. He wrote one novel in lyrical prose, *The Notebooks of Malte Laurids Brigge (Die Aufzeichnungen des Malte Laurids Brigge)*, but mostly wrote verse, although he is also known for his several collections of his voluminous correspondence. Rilke's work is often considered to be mystical, and his imagery often focuses on the challenge of being in communion with the ineffable—especially in what W. H. Auden termed "the age of anxiety."

Rilke is also known for his contributions to French literature for his having written over 400 poems, originally written in French, and dedicated to the canton of Valais, in Switzerland. However, he is more renowned for his collections of poetry, written toward the end of his life, *Duino Elegies (Duineser Elegien)* and *Sonnets to Orpheus (Die Sonette an Orpheus)*, as well as the posthumously collected *Letters to a Young Poet (Briefe an einen jungen Dichter)*.

In the early 20th century, a century after his death, Rilke is still one of the more popular and best-selling poets, whose work is also qualitatively and distinctly accomplished.

He is also known for having chosen a poem he wrote for his epitaph, which bears a motif that can be found throughout his work, and that being the image of the rose, in all of its variations. The poem on his gravestone in the churchyard of Raron, Switzerland reads:

> Rose, oh reiner Widerspruch, Lust,
> Niemandes Schlaf zu sein unter soviel
> Lidern.
>
> —Rainer Maria Rilke

> Rose, o pure contradiction, desire
> To be the sleep that no one wants
> Under so many lids

Wally Swist's *Huang Po and the Dimensions of Love* (Southern Illinois University Press, 2012) was selected by Yusef Komunyakaa as co-winner in the 2011 Crab Orchard Series Open Poetry Contest. He was the 2018 winner of the Ex Ophidia Press Poetry Prize, by unanimous judging, for his collection *A Bird Who Seems to Know Me: Poetry Regarding Birds and Nature* (2019). Recent books include *Awakening and Visitation* (2020), *Evanescence: Selected Poems* (2020), and *Taking Residence* (2021), all with Shanti Arts.

His books of nonfiction include *Singing for Nothing: Selected Nonfiction as Literary Memoir* (Brooklyn, NY: The Operating System, 2018), *On Beauty: Essays, Reviews, Fiction, and Plays* (New York & Lisbon: Adelaide Books, 2018), and *A Writer's Statements on Beauty: New and Selected Essays and Reviews* (Brunswick, ME: Shanti Arts, 2022). His translation of L'Allegria by Giuseppe Ungaretti was published by Shanti Arts in 2023.

Swist is a recipient of Artist's Fellowships in poetry from the Connecticut Commission on the Arts (1977 and 2003).

His essays, poetry, and translations have appeared in *Asymptote* (Taiwan), *Chicago Quarterly Review, Commonweal, Ezra: An Online Journal of Translation, Healing Muse, Hunger Mountain, La Piccioletta Barca* (U.K.), *The Montreal Review, Poetry London, Today's American Catholic, Transference: A Literary Journal Featuring the Art & Process of Translation, (Western Michigan Department of Languages), Vox Populi,* and *Your Impossible Voice*.

His book, *Aperture*, poems regarding caregiving his spouse through Alzheimer's, was published in 2025 by Kelsay Books.

Wild Rose Bush: The Life of Mary and Other Poems by Rainer Maria Rilke was selected as an honorable mention in the 2025 Stephen Mitchell Prize for Excellence in Translation sponsored by Green Linden Press.

www.ingramcontent.com/pod-product-compliance
Lightning Source LLC
Chambersburg PA
CBHW030056170426
43197CB00010B/1546